WHY PEOPLE DON'T LIKE YOU

Bramnick's Guide to Interpersonal Skills

By Jon Bramnick

www.funniestlawyernewjersey.com

DEDICATION

This book is dedicated to my parents
Herb and Babette Bramnick.

Special thanks to Pat Brentano, Brent and Abigail Bramnick,
Vinnie Brand, Mike Duhaime, Daryl Isherwood, Lisa Hetfield,
David Shane, Bob Kraus, Rosemary Bauer, Bobby Gregory,
Earl "the Pearl" Monroe, James Scott Bramnick,
Governor Chris Christie, Chris Porrino, Senator Jeff Chiesa,
Tom Kean, Jr., Bill Palatucci, Harold Poltrock, Michele Albano,
Jack Bilman, Jeff Miller, Pat Toscano, Mark Duffy,
Mayor Andrew Skibitsky, John Rochford, Vic Richel,
Joe Piscopo, Laura Ali, Jeff O'Connor,
Ben Demarzo, and Myra Mata.

GRATITUDE

I would like to express my deep gratitude and appreciation to Jonathan Holtz, who not only did a fantastic job putting this book together, but is also an outstanding trial attorney at my firm. Behind every great man is a great woman, his wife Amanda, and their son William, the light of their life.

FOREWARD

As a politician, comedian, and trial lawyer, I have had the opportunity to observe thousands of people in many different settings. Interpersonal skills are extremely important to be successful. This book provides over 200 simple and very clear rules that should assist you in your day to day interaction with people.

As a comedian, I studied how to make people laugh. As a lawyer, I learned how to persuade people to agree with me. As a politician, I worked hard to try to get people to like me.

This book attempts to take all of those experiences and condense them into "Bramnick's Guide to Interpersonal Skills."

I hope you enjoy reading the rules of the road… Please note, I still violate these rules.

Don't hurt me when you shake my hand, Hercules.

Whoever told you that a firm handshake was squeezing the hell out of someone's hand was nuts. If you are in good shape, I promise I will notice.

Rule 1

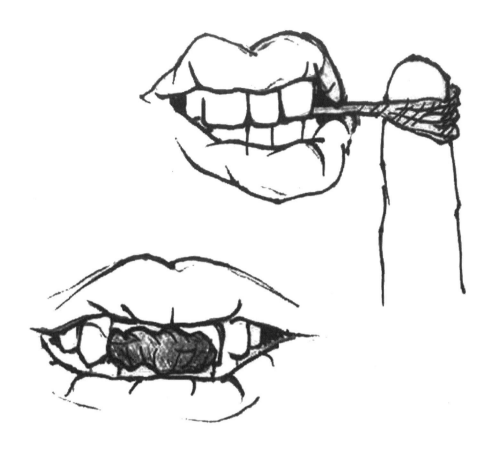

Chewing gum never looks good.

Unless you are playing left field for the
Yankees. Hiding the gum in your cheek
looks worse, and I'll see it anyway.

Rule 2

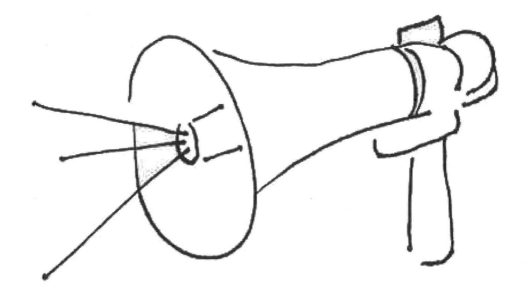

Never start a story with "What most people don't know..."

You're telling me you know
more than everyone else.

Rule 3

Don't say "I have a funny story to tell you."

Just tell the story and let
the audience decide.

Rule 4

Someone's name is music to their ears.

Remembering someone's name is well worth the effort. If you forget someone's name, try covering with "sir," "boss," "pal," or "brother."

Rule 5

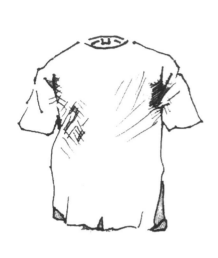

Wearing a dirty Mickey Mouse shirt on a plane is not going to impress a client.

You may be comfortable, but a potential or existing client will not love it. I wear a tie and jacket when traveling on an airline, and I get instant respect from flight attendants and sometimes even TSA.

Rule 6

**Mentioning your Ivy League school
in every conversation is annoying.**

When I say "How are you?" and you say
"I just got back from vacation with my
roommate from Princeton." Interesting, you
went to college 40 years ago and
all you wanted to do was mention
your Ivy League credential. BAD.

Rule 7

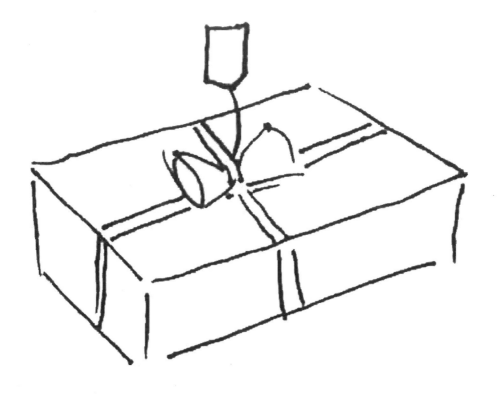

**When I invite you to my house
and tell you not to bring anything,
bring something.**

Rule 8

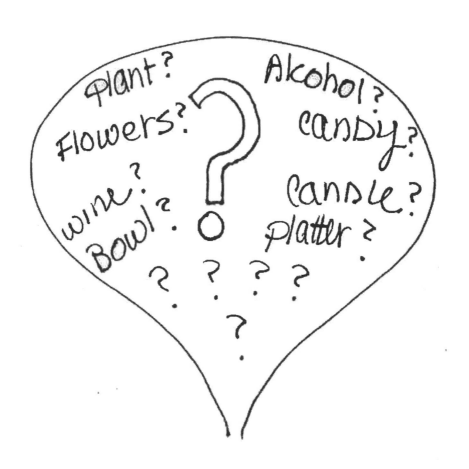

Don't ask the host what you can bring.

Otherwise you're asking me to
choose my own gift.

Rule 9

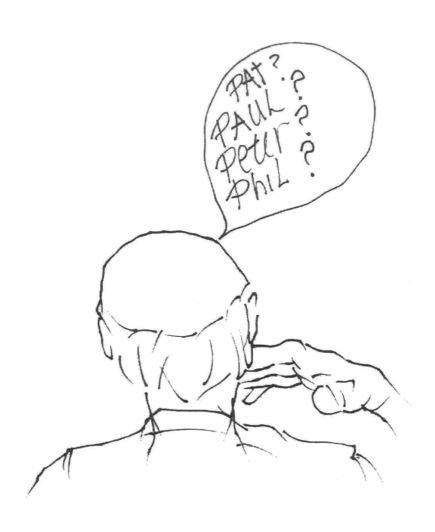

If you think someone doesn't know your name, just roll with it.

Don't embarrass them by saying
"You don't know my name?"

Rule 10

**It is not helpful to mention
you were friendly 25 years ago with
somebody of the same ethnicity.**

The hearer will pick up on the fact that you
see only ethnicity. Example: When speaking
to a Jewish person, don't try to ingratiate
yourself by saying "One of my best friends
in college was David Goldberg."

Rule 11

When meeting a politician, ask a question rather than give an opinion.

People tend to explode with an opinion because this is their opportunity to tell the elected official what they have been thinking about for years. Your time is better spent asking the elected official what their opinion is on that topic, then explaining your own opinion.

Rule 12

If you are starting a new business, don't have voicemail.

Either use your cell phone or
a live answering company.

Rule 13

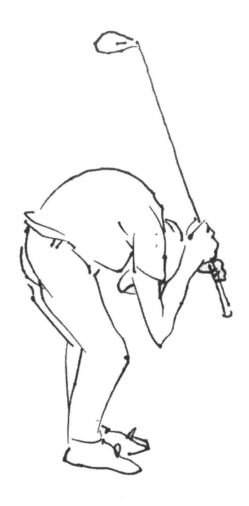

Don't make excuses about your golf game when you are playing poorly.

Nobody gives a shit, and they don't believe you anyway. Your game speaks for itself.

Rule 14

Follow the Mark Duffy Rule.

Don't be more trouble than you're worth.
You may be a genius, but if you are too big
of a pain in the ass, you won't make it.

Rule 15

Follow the Lisa Hetfield Rule.

No one ever got in trouble
by saying too little.

Rule 16

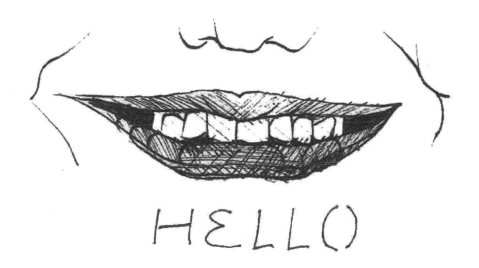

HELLO

Follow the Jack Bilman Rule.

A smile and a hello is always good.

Rule 17

Follow the David Shane Rule.

I asked my friend and excellent lawyer Dave Shane why his interpersonal skills are so good, and he responded, "I just listen."

Rule 18

Egos cost money.

If your business decision is
based on your ego, it will cost you.

Rule 19

It is amazing how much can be accomplished when you are not worried about who gets the credit.

Let success be your reward,
not credit for doing your job.

Rule 20

The only people who care about your success are your mom and dad.

Bragging to other people about your
success is not helpful. Let your
achievements speak for themselves.

Rule 21

Ignore insults unless you absolutely have to respond.

Ignoring a stupid comment is
torture to the person attacking you.
Silence is how you embarrass the speaker
because you don't think he is
worth a response.

Rule 22

Grudges are a complete waste of time, and they consume energy needed to be successful.

Get over it.

Rule 23

When answering an office phone, never say "Hold on."

Instead, say "May I place you on hold while I connect you to Mr Smith?" or "Sorry to place you on hold; I will find Mr. Smith for you."

Rule 24

When working in a store, a clerk should not say "Next" to a line of customers.

"May I help you? I'm sorry for the wait,"
lets customers know they're valued.
Also, clerks should talk to the people in line
and say "Thank you for waiting."
Clerks should not be talking to other clerks
while I am patiently waiting to be served.
Also acknowledge and say "Hello" to people
sitting in the waiting room.

Rule 25

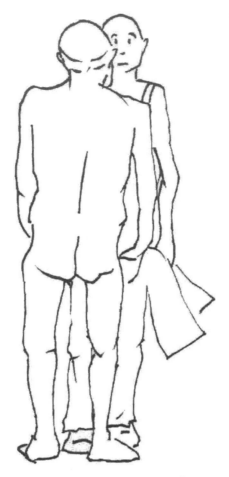

If I see you in the locker room, wrap yourself in a towel, Pops.

Towels are easily accessible in the men's locker room. Get one. Whoever told you walking around a locker room in your birthday suit was okay must have been a weirdo.

Rule 26

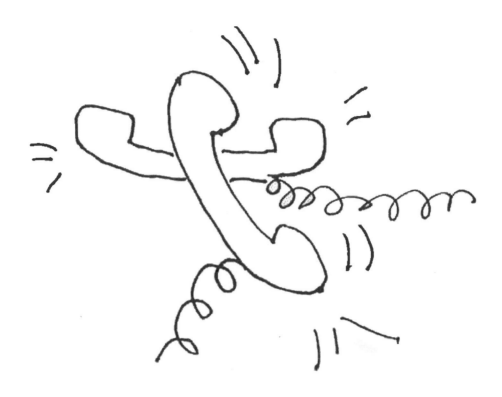

Follow the Bob Kraus Rule.

Bob was diagnosed with lung cancer and never smoked. He told me if a friend receives a bad diagnosis or suffers a loss and you are not sure if you should call, CALL. I understand it is a difficult call; that is exactly why the call is important.

Rule 27

Remember the
Herbert X. Bramnick Rule

If you look too closely at your friends, you
will end up not having any. All of us will be
disappointed by a friend's words or actions.
We also make mistakes. If you want friends
exactly like you, your only friend will be
the person in the mirror.

Rule 28

★ ★ ★ ★ ★

thai   ITALIAN   FRENCH   JAPANESE
ᴊᴴᴸ   ᴊᴴᴸ   ᴊᴴᴸ   ᴊᴴᴸ

Don't play "Can you top this?" with restaurants.

If your friend tells you Pepe's is his favorite restaurant, the proper response is "Thank you, I'll try it," NOT "No, the best Italian restaurant is Cosimo's." Why not let the speaker enjoy the moment?

Rule 29

When out to dinner with another person, take the bad seat with no view.

Especially if you are the first to arrive at the restaurant.

Rule 30

When the waiter hands you a menu, don't bury your face in it immediately.

Continue your conversation, then order. You are out for dinner with friends, and the purpose is to talk to your friends or business guests you have invited. The menu is not going anywhere, but your guests may the next time they receive your invite.

Rule 31

Follow the
"Quick Draw McGraw" Rule.

Returning calls quickly is a reliable path
to success. While waiting for your call, the
client or customer found someone else.
You should return the call quickly even if it
is to say "Sorry, I cannot speak right now,
but I will get back to you this afternoon."

Rule 32

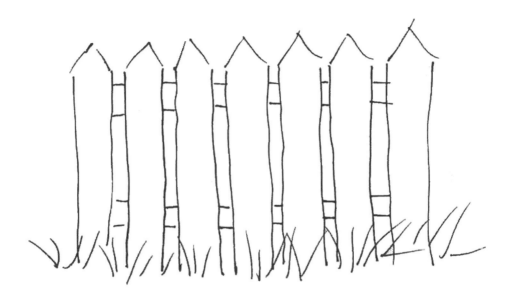

One bad relationship has multiple effects on your ability to be successful.

That one person you had a serious conflict with is advertising against you at no charge. People talk about other people all the time. You do not want all that bad publicity.

Rule 33

You ROCK!
WAY to GO!
GOOD JOb!
Well done!

Compliments are always good.

Telling others good things about themselves
is always a good thing.
"You look great."
"You have been a great friend."

Rule 34

Send thank you notes for everything.

People like to be appreciated.
A short note goes a long way. An email or
a text are good—a handwritten note
might be even better!

Rule 35

Do not correct people or your spouse regarding details that are not important.

"It was Tuesday afternoon at 4:00 p.m."
"No it wasn't, Dear, it was 6:00 p.m." The interruption of the story has no importance other than to interrupt your spouse and makes you look like a pain in the ass.

Rule 36

**When I ask you how was your golf
game, it is a throw-away question.**

I don't need a play-by-play of every shot you
hit. A proper response is "Some good, some
bad," or "I had a good day."

Rule 37

When stopping at my table at a restaurant, in your own mind hum the Jeopardy theme song. When it is over, move on.

We are being polite by listening to you, but we would like to eat. You are simply walking by someone's table. It is polite to stop and say hello; it is not polite to spend 10 minutes hovering over them.

Rule 38

If you have nothing to say, say it.

Do not try to get into a conversation
unless you have something to add.
Everyone knows the saying "It is better to
be silent and thought a fool than to speak
and remove all doubt."

Rule 39

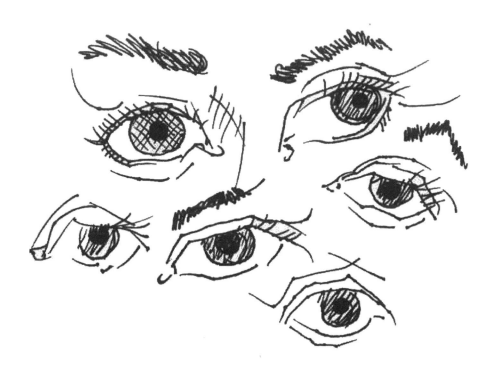

Eye contact, eye contact, eye contact.

Do not look over my shoulder for
the most important person in the room.
Locking your eyes on the person speaking
is really, really important.

Rule 40

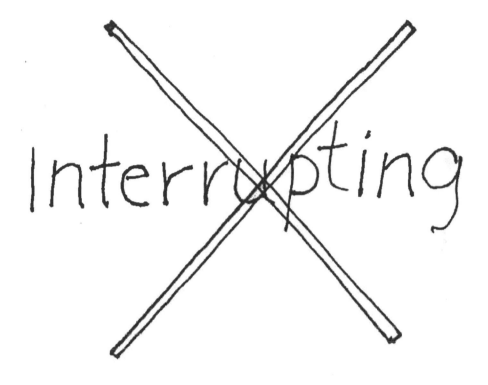

Don't say "Sorry to interrupt" if you are interrupting for no real reason.

Just WAIT until the people are finished with their discussion. Only interrupt if there is a fire.

Rule 41

Don't post photos on social media from parties where others may not have been invited.

You were invited to a "private" party.
That is what "private" means.
The host now has to explain to someone why they were not invited because you told the world. Brag about something else.

Rule 42

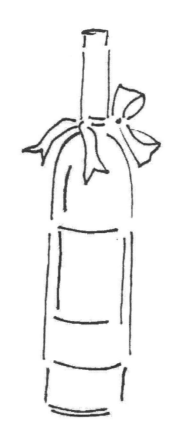

If you come to my house and bring wine, don't insist that I open it.

If you do, the wine is no longer a gift, it is wine you brought to drink. If you must drink your wine, bring two bottles. Unfortunately, you are telling the host you only drink certain wine.

Rule 43

**The social and business environments
are a nebulous web,
so be nice to everyone.**

It is a small world, and it is amazing who
knows who. If you are nice to everyone,
it will work out very well.

Rule 44

**It takes five years to build trust
and five minutes to lose it.**

Your reputation for honesty and integrity is
extremely important. Never, ever,
do anything that could place your
reputation in jeopardy.

Rule 45

DINNER PARTIES

us	them

Follow the Mrs. Bauer Rule.

Being overly generous is never a bad thing.
My friend Mrs. Bauer invited me
to a very nice dinner party. I told her,
"We will have to invite you back to our
house," and she replied, "I don't keep
count." Your generosity will serve you
very well in the long term.

Rule 46

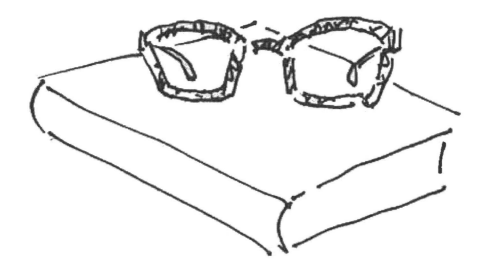

Don't ask me "Did you read DJ Smith's novel?"

Your purpose is to tell me you read a novel.
Great. Just tell me about the book.
If I read it, I will let you know.
Why ask me the question?

Rule 47

**If someone asks you for help,
don't say "If you run for governor,
I will help you."**

How about helping me now?

Rule 48

Don't ask "How are 'we' doing?"

I can only make a call on how I am doing.
The question has some "coldness" to it.

Rule 49

**Avoid "mentionitis"—The annoying
act of mentioning stuff to impress me.**

Repeatedly talking about your cars, homes,
and successful investments
doesn't make you sound successful.
It makes you sound insecure.
If you are a success, I will figure it out.

Rule 50

Be very careful about repeatedly canceling appointments or social engagements.

Eventually others will realize
there is a pattern.

Rule 51

Don't place your hand on
the rim of my cup.

Rule 52

If I spend half an hour giving you free advice, don't end the conversation by telling me that's what you were thinking all along.

A good response is "Thank you for your help, I really appreciate it."

Rule 53

Follow the "20/10 Rule" in the office.

When you or an employee walk by a customer or client in a business environment, smile when you're 20 feet away. If you are within 10 feet, say hello. Ignoring the customer or client makes no sense. I learned this rule when I visited St. Barnabas Hospital in New Jersey.

Rule 54

When you're working out at the gym, please limit the moans, groans, and sighs! Please try, my friend.

There are people who work out and insist on making sure everyone in the gym knows how hard they are working out. ANNOYING.

Rule 55

If you are calling me, NEVER, EVER, have your secretary call me and say "Hold on for Mr. Smith," unless you are the president of the United States.

Listen here Mr. Busy, I am busy also.

Rule 56

People in your waiting room
SHOULD NOT WAIT.

I understand it is a waiting room, yet if I am there on time, you should be ready to see me even if you are a doctor. If you must make me wait, apologize and explain why.

Rule 57

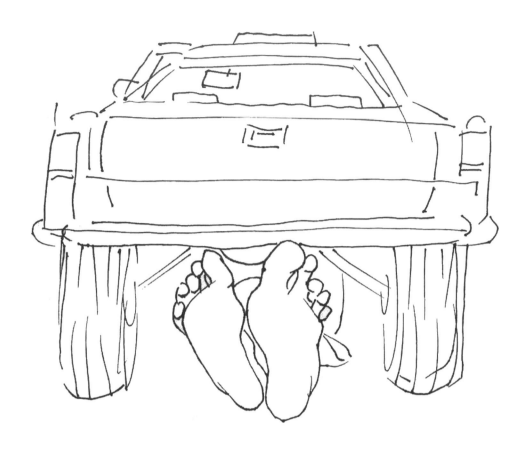

Never, ever, be late. Unless you were run over by a truck.

I made sure to leave 15 minutes early so I would not inconvenience you, and your excuse? I hope it is not traffic in New Jersey. That should be in your plans.

Rule 58

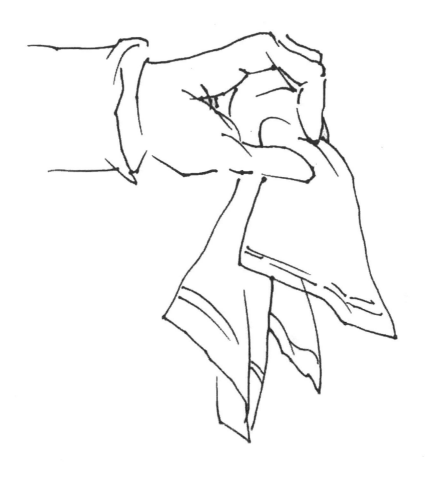

Empathy is essential.

You do not have to compare your own story. Just say "I am so sorry." Someone lost their job; do not tell your own story, just express your concern, or say "How can I help?"

Rule 59

If someone asks you to say a few words, they mean a few words.

Make them laugh, make them cry, say goodbye. You are not a keynote speaker.

Rule 60

Shocking news: People may not like your perfume or cologne.

Wear it at home, not at the office. When you hug and kiss me, now I have to smell your perfume for the rest of the evening.

Rule 61

Regrets to an invitation should come from you, not your assistant.

Bad: "On behalf of Senator Jones, he will not be able to attend your party." Okay, big shot. On behalf of Jon Bramnick, he will not be voting for Senator Jones.

Rule 62

Don't overstay your welcome when invited to someone's home.

Try to get a sense of whether it is late
for the hosts. If they start cleaning up...
Read the signs, Mr. Tone Deaf.

Rule 63

When you're in a conversation, the most important thing you can do is ask questions.

It's not always all about you.

Rule 64

Store clerks who say "Have a nice day" in a monotone make it crystal clear they don't give a damn.

If you have the job, try to at least fake it.

Rule 65

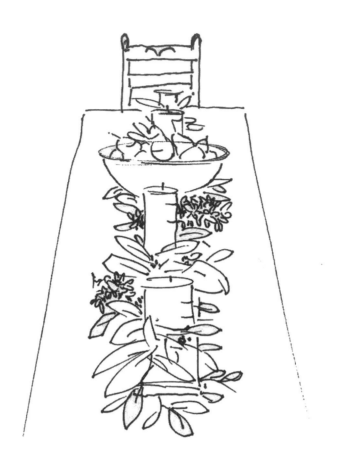

The host should spend as much time planning the conversation as he or she does in planning the menu.

Table questions are good. If you don't plan a table conversation, the side conversations may be very boring.

Rule 66

**For my many friends who do
a shake and a hug, I am good with
the guy-to-guy hug as long as it
follows the anti-Hercules rule:
Do not squeeze me, just a symbolic
hug with minimal contact.**

The stronger squeeze does not
indicate to me you like me any more,
Mr. Bruno Sammartino.

Rule 67

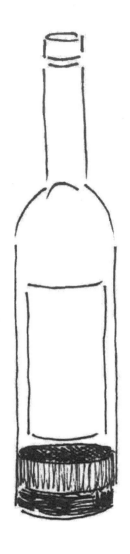

**Always offer the last glass of wine
in the bottle to your guests.**

Even if it's a bottle you've been saving,
you're still the host. Guests come first.

Rule 68

If someone invites you to their favorite restaurant, don't tell them your meal was "so-so."

It's their favorite for a reason. Whether you loved it or not, tell them you did.

Rule 69

If invited with your children to a friend's house, don't let them run wild.

Just because your kids jump on the furniture in your house doesn't mean your hosts will be okay with it. Even if you believe children should not be disciplined, it does not work at my house.

Rule 70

Don't be the person who always brings up politics and religion at parties.

Conversations can quickly get out of control and soon your friends will be partying without you.

Rule 71

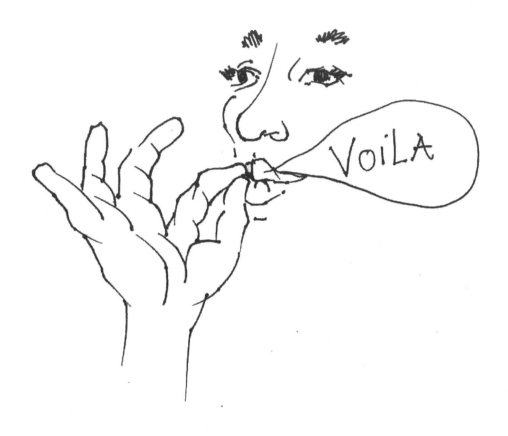

Always rave about the host's cooking.

If you're invited for dinner and the host
cooks, the food was "phenomenal,"
"delicious," or "wonderful." Period.

Rule 72

**Don't play "I can top that!"
with your kid's accomplishments.**

If you friend tells you his son
was accepted to Rutgers, the right answer
is "Congratulations! You must be proud,"
not "My daughter is a shoe-in
for Princeton."

Rule 73

**Treat waitstaff with respect
and tip well.**

Nothing screams of self-importance
like being rude to a waiter
and skimping on the tip.

Rule 74

**Don't offer your advice
if you're not asked.**

If I want advice, I promise I'll ask you.
Otherwise, you're just telling me
what to do.

Rule 75

If you're asked to give a eulogy, talk about the decedent, not YOU.

When I was at Yale with my friend, Bob (the decedent), he was the first person to help me when I ran for class president. My term as president at Yale was always supported by Bob. I would not be a CEO today of a large corporation but for Bob. I will miss Bob.

Rule 76

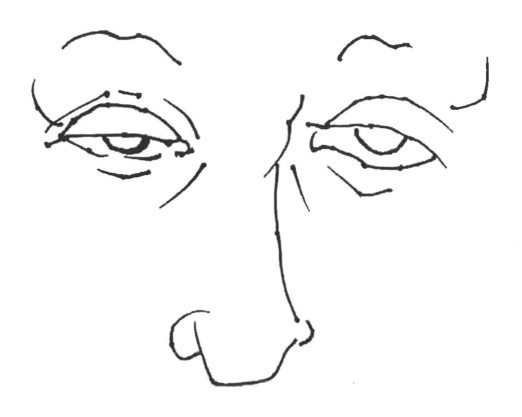

**Never tell anyone they look tired
unless you are their mom
or their doctor.**

Basically, you are telling them they look
bad, so keep your opinion to yourself.

Rule 77

THANK YOU

MERCI BEAUCOUP

GRACIAS

DANKE SEHR

GRAZIE

When someone compliments you, say "Thank you."

No need to either explain or comment.

Rule 78

If someone sends you business, you should always pass along your gratitude.

A good line is "I am very grateful for your referral." You may want to send a small token of your appreciation.

Rule 79

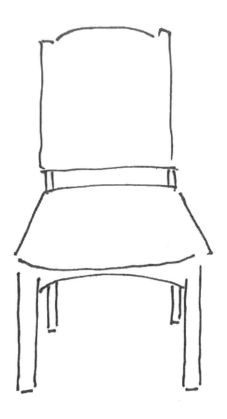

**Your employees should never say
to a client or customer "Take a seat."**

Instead, a good practice is to say
"Mr. Bramnick will be right with you.
May I get you some coffee?"
A chair speaks for itself; people know
how to use it if they wish.

Rule 80

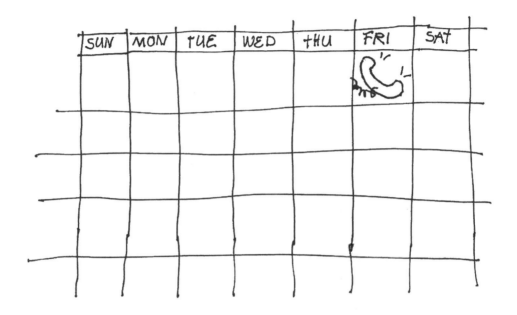

If you say "I will call you tomorrow," **CALL THE PERSON TOMORROW, MR. BUSY, OR DON'T SAY IT.**

Rule 81

Don't dominate the host or hostess's time; there are others who would like to talk to them.

This also applies to the
famous person at the event.

Rule 82

If a client calls you and is upset, apologize.

Simply say "I am very sorry."
APOLOGIZE, STUPID, AND YOU WILL
GET OFF THE PHONE SOONER.
Plus you may keep the client.

Rule 83

**Don't start eating until everyone
is served, Big Foot.**

If you don't know this rule,
don't waste your time learning
more about interpersonal skills.

Rule 84

Don't look over a person's shoulder to see who else is in the room.

Your dinner companion should get your full attention. Don't insult them by looking to see who else is around.

Rule 85

When you walk in front of someone, say "Excuse me."

This is a very old rule,
but is still important.

Rule 86

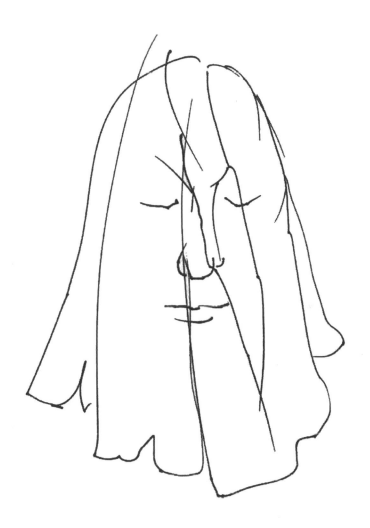

Thinly veiled criticism is just that.

When you say "I really like what you did,
and it could have been even better if you
had (fill in the blank)," you send
a clear and critical message.

Rule 87

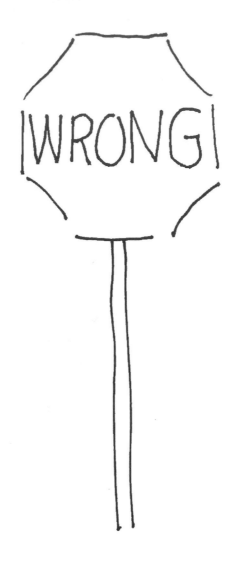

**Good leaders know we are
never so sure of ourselves
as when we are dead wrong.**

Rule 88

Your accomplishments and superior knowledge aren't nearly as impressive as your humility and self-deprecation.

Rule 89

**Let the person in line behind you
with one item go ahead of you.**

You're never in too much of a hurry
to be polite.

Rule 90

When heading to a meeting or an appointment, leave 30 minutes early.

That way, when you bump into a friend or client, you have time to speak to them and still be on time.

Rule 91

Follow the Pat Toscano Rule.

Always ring the doorbell with your elbows.
Your hands should be full of gifts.

Rule 92

Don't place your drink on someone's wooden table.

It makes a mark, dummy.

Rule 93

Don't ask me in your house "What would you like to drink?"

Instead, show me what you are offering,
otherwise I may ask you for
a drink you don't have.

Rule 94

Scotch

1. The Glenlivet
2. The Balvenie
3. Dewar's
4. Jonnie Walker
5. Highland Park

**Don't say you have scotch
without telling me the brand.**

**If I am the first guest,
don't bring me a bottle of wine
that was opened yesterday.**

Open a new bottle. Your guests will
appreciate it, and you won't look cheap.

Rule 96

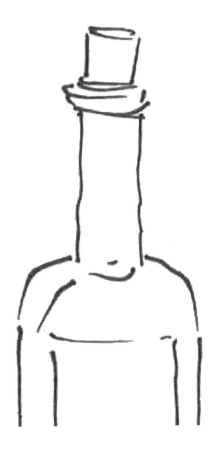

**When you invite someone to
a dinner party, DO NOT insist
they taste the dessert.**

They may have just started a diet
or may have food allergies.
Let the person decide without pressure.

Rule 97

Hold the door open for the person behind you, or for someone who walks in at the same time.

It only takes a few seconds to wait, but it makes a good impression.

Rule 98

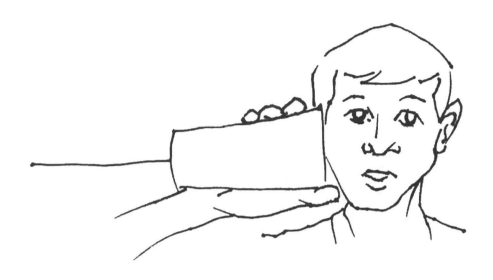

Make sure you hang up your cell phone before talking badly about me.

Feel free to trash me,
but I don't need to hear it.

Rule 99

**If your hands are sweaty, dry them off
before you shake my hand.
If you sneeze into your hand,
please don't shake hands with me.**

After we shake, I don't want a soaking wet
hand, or worse, a cold. Dry your hand,
or tell me you're sick, so you're not able to
shake. I promise I won't be offended.

Rule 100

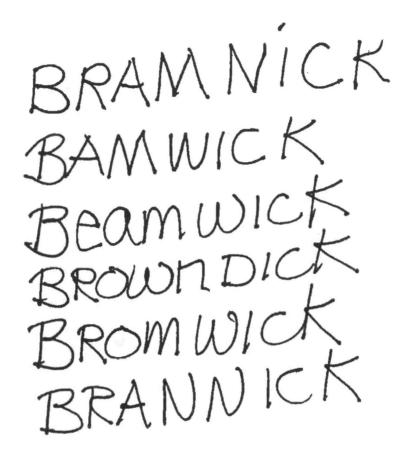

When you introduce me, please pronounce my name correctly.

If I have to correct you,
it embarrasses us both.

Rule 101

Always leave a message—a short one.

Don't make me listen to your
long, meandering message. And don't
race through your phone number so
fast that I cannot understand it.

Rule 102

**Never start a call you made
with "Who's this?"**

If you don't know, you shouldn't be calling.

Rule 103

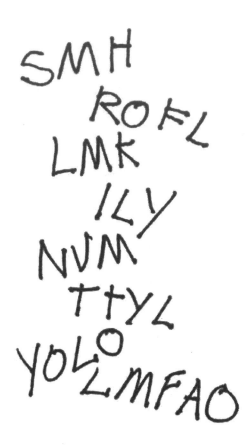

When texting or emailing, don't use two letters when five will do.

You're not curing cancer in the five seconds you saved by typing "TY."

Rule 104

Never use "lol" in a business message.

Chances are they are not even
laughing on the inside.

Rule 105

Don't say "I didn't get the call."

It never looks good.
I paid $1,000 for my phone too,
and the history feature always works.

Rule 106

WAR
and
PEACE

LEO TOLSTOY

Texts are for short messages.

Save War and Peace for an email.
Come to think of it, don't email me
War and Peace either.

Rule 107

If you cut someone off when driving, have the decency to wave and acknowledge that you were the one in the wrong.

It goes a long way to diffuse road rage.

Rule 108

**When driving, put down the phone.
No texting, no Facebook,
no Instagram.**

And while we are at it, the car is not for
your makeup, shaving, breakfast,
or shelling a bag of pistachios.

Rule 109

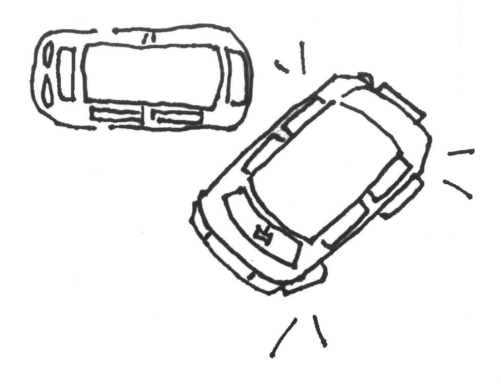

Never cut anyone off in the parking lot.

You will inevitably be standing behind that person in five minutes, regardless of your destination. Even worse, they might be sitting across from you in the interview you were rushing to get to.

Rule 110

Clean your car.

You never know when you will have to give someone a ride, and there will never be a good way to explain the Whopper wrapper on the floor after all your talk of "juicing and clean living."

Rule 111

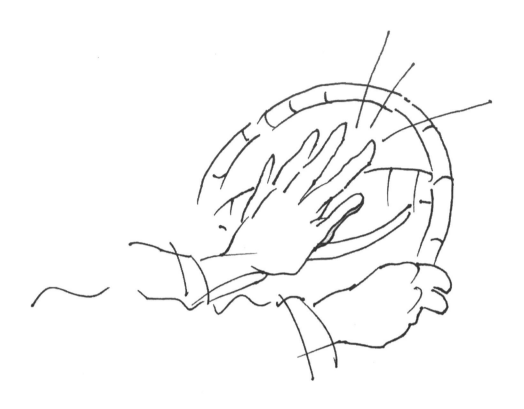

Learn the levels of honking
when the light changes.

Short bursts are meant to alert other drivers;
sitting on the horn just means
you're an asshole.

Rule 112

Stop driving aggressively.

You know that 99% of the time
I will end up sitting right next to you
at the next red light. I'll be the one
with the big grin on my face, and brakes
that will still work in six months.

Rule 113

Don't cover your car in stickers.

You just advised the world how many
kids you have, where they have their after-
school activities, the size of your dog,
and your hometown...sleep tight.
Congrats, you were at "South of the Border."
That is quite an accomplishment.

Rule 114

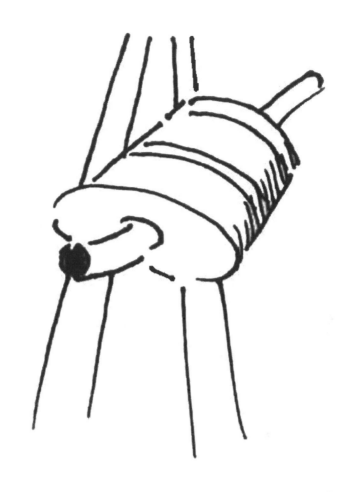

Get your car checked out.

I can hear your muffler is about to fall off.
While you might not care, I would rather
not be behind you when it happens.

Rule 115

**When someone takes you to dinner,
don't order the five-pound lobster.**

Order cheap.

Rule 116

When you meet someone for the first time and you are introduced, it is extremely important to look the person in the eye and say "Really pleased to meet you."

Don't mumble "Hi" while looking at your shoes.

Rule 117

Don't ever be the underdressed person at the party or meeting.

Underdressing works for rockstars and tech moguls, not for the rest of us.

Rule 118

If you say hi to a friend while he's out with his wife, don't ignore her while you two talk about your last golf outing.

If you want to stay friends,
ALWAYS say hello to the spouse,
even if you've never met.

Rule 119

Reach deep when tipping the shoe guy, valet people, or others.

You can do better than $1, Mr. Cheapskates. Keep in mind workers talk to other works and management, especially if you joined a fancy club. Figure another way to save money.

Rule 120

When you board a plane, don't smack people with your backpack or briefcase.

Be aware of your surroundings.
There are 200 other people
squeezing into the same small space.

Rule 121

**Don't tell people you won money
in Atlantic City, asshole.**

Most people you know have lost a lot more
than you have won over the years.

Rule 122

A strong ego is good.
A big ego is bad.

Rule 123

Never ask a woman if she is pregnant.

If she is, she'll tell you if she wants to.
If she isn't, you just called some
poor woman overweight.

Rule 124

Don't give golf lessons, bowling lessons, or tennis instructions to anyone unless they ask.

If the person wants your help,
they will ask.

Rule 125

Shoes should be shined often.

Don't let your shoes get dirty and scuffed. If
you can't keep your shoes clean,
how can you handle my case?

Rule 126

**If you want to keep a secret,
don't tell anybody.**

Rule 127

Don't skimp on clothes.

Often your suit will be the first thing a new
client or acquaintance notices. Your clothing
budget is not the place to save money.

Rule 128

Don't talk badly about people when they aren't around.

Whomever you're talking to is inevitably left wondering what you say about them when they are not around.

Rule 129

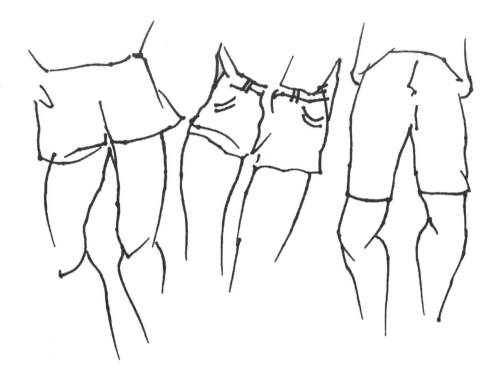

Your boss should set the dress code.

If your boss doesn't wear shorts to work,
you should not either.

Rule 130

**If you were wrong,
admit it quickly and apologize.**

Everybody is wrong sometimes.
It's how you handle it
that sets you apart.

Rule 131

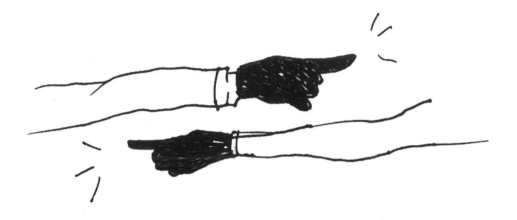

Don't blame others for your failures.

It makes you look petty,
and people will not believe you anyway.
It is probably not their fault.

Rule 132

**Designated drivers
DON'T DRINK AT ALL.**

Is that so difficult to understand?

Rule 133

If you introduce a person to your friend, provide information to the person about your friend.

Joe is a surgeon at the local hospital.

Rule 134

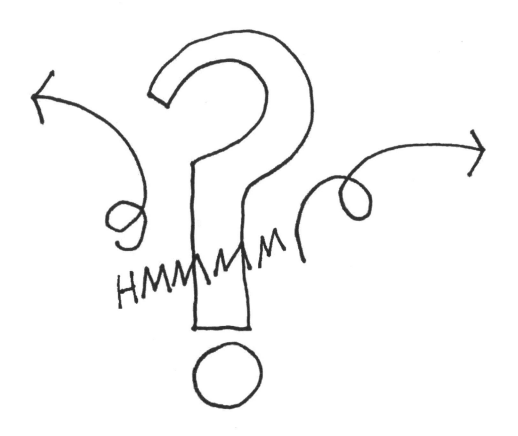

Don't use "terms of art."

If people aren't in your business, they
won't know what you're talking about.
This applies also to your discussion of
your sailboat. "You know the jib, the port,
and the starboard when you jibe."

Rule 135

bring/take you/I
I/me this/which
Farther/Further

Don't use words if you're not 100% sure what they mean.

Using words incorrectly—
or mispronouncing them—
hurts your credibility.

Rule 136

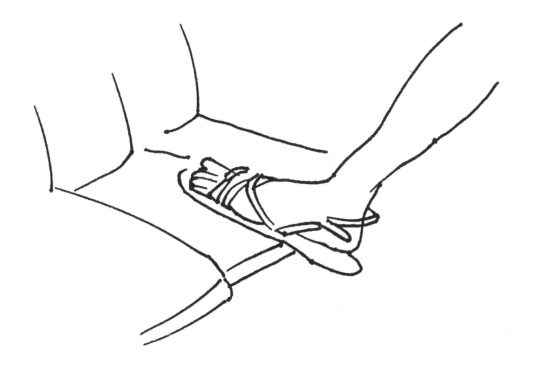

Keep your feet off the seats of public transportation.

Nobody wants to wear your footprints on their pants.

Rule 137

**Ordering donuts is not
a major life decision.**

They're all good. Just pick one and move on.
The people behind you will thank you.

Rule 138

When you give someone a compliment, don't qualify it.

"You look great," NOT "You look great for having had four kids."

Rule 139

**Speed it up in the crosswalk,
Mr. Important.**

Pick up the pace, just a little.

Rule 140

Drop something off to welcome a new family or person to the neighborhood or building.

Even a box of cookies will do.
But don't just drop it off,
include a NOTE!

Rule 141

When you answer the phone for someone, don't ask "Who's calling?" or "The reason for the call?"

Instead say "May I ask who's calling?" and "Will he know what this is about?"

Rule 142

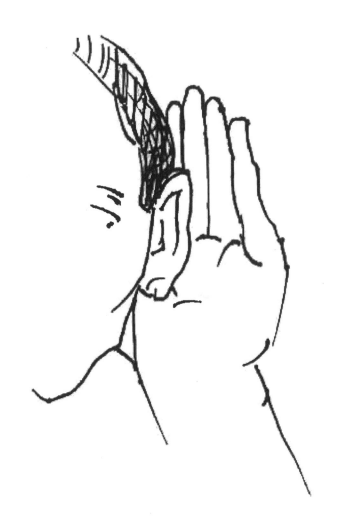

Try to understand
rather than be understood.

Sometimes it's better to listen
than to be heard.

Rule 143

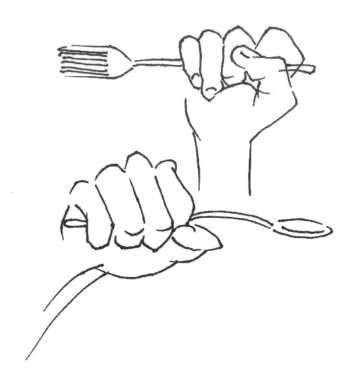

**Pay attention to your table manners.
Trust me, you're being judged on them.**

Don't slurp your coffee. Don't smack your
lips or chew with your mouth open.
And for the love of God, don't pick up
your soup to drink the last drop like you're
camping in the Poconos. If the spoon
can't get it, leave it in the bowl.

Rule 144

Don't drink out of the stir stick.

Just because it has a hole doesn't make it a straw. It is a tiny plastic stick in your cocktail. It looks stupid in your mouth.

Rule 145

If someone is telling you about their favorite TV show, don't respond with "I never watch television."

We get it, you're way too smart
for that, Einstein.

Rule 146

Pick your specialty license plate carefully.*

Nobody cares that you're a dentist. They only sort of care that you're GREATGUY2, and they definitely don't care that you're a Knicks fan. If you're supporting a cause like curing cancer, than go for it.

*The sad thing is the author has a personalized plate.

Rule 147

If you're having me over for dinner, have options for the food.

What if I don't eat fish?

Rule 148

**Cars should share the road
with bicyclists.**

But if you're riding a bike, don't ride three
across bullshitting about the weather or
what great shape you're in.

Rule 149

If you miss your exit, miss it.

Don't back up on the highway, moron.

Rule 150

HAVE — A — NICE — DAY

Do not rush through "Have a nice day" so fast that it doesn't mean shit except that you were told to say it.

If you're saying it, try to mean it.

Rule 151

Don't ever argue about youth sports.

If you're yelling at the ref at an 8-year-old's basketball game, you need psychiatric help.

Rule 152

Teach your children to say "please" and "thank you."

Even though they're kids, lack of basic manners reflects on you.

Rule 153

Remember birthdays, anniversaries, and special occasions, especially for employees.

Nothing says you care like remembering a friend's or colleague's birthday.

Rule 154

Never badmouth your spouse or partner to your friends.

Even if others are doing it or you are
in the middle of a fight, respect
your spouse enough not to
trash them in public.

Rule 155

Don't gloat when you win.

Rule 156

Don't ever comment on a woman's appearance in a business setting.

It's a business meeting, she's there to do business, not to look good for you.

Rule 157

Don't swear in a business meeting.

Cursing is fine when you're golfing
with your buddies, not when you're
negotiating a contract.

Rule 158

**Listen closely to other peoples'
needs and comments.**

They are serious requests even if said in jest.

Rule 159

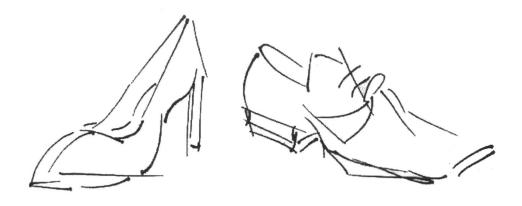

If a guest asks you where the restroom is, walk them halfway if the directions are complicated.

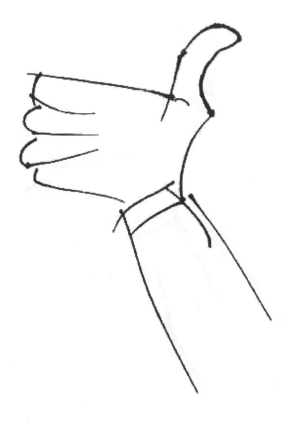

Overreact to invitations to golf, parties, etc.

Even if you don't plan to attend, your positive reaction will make them happy they invited you. Example: "Thank you so much for the invite, I really appreciate it. Unfortunately, I am out of state."

Rule 161

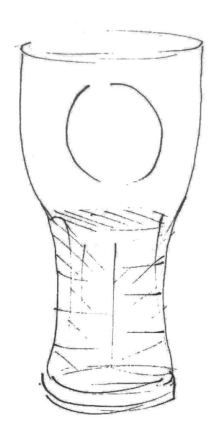

Follow the Bobby Gregory Rule on country club social sports.

My friend Bobby Gregory says losing is easier than beating a friend.
"It takes half a beer to get over a loss and three days to get over a win."

Rule 162

Walk your dog with a leash.

I know you think you're the dog whisperer,
but I may not love your dog. It's also the law.

Rule 163

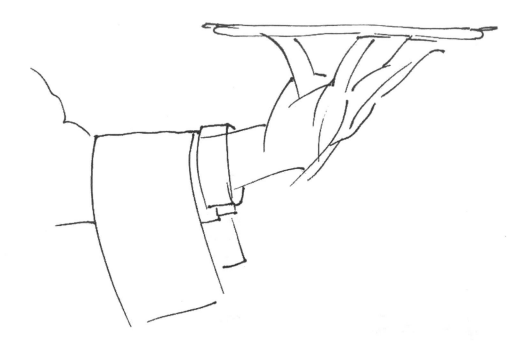

If you are a waitress or waiter, repeat the order back to the customer.

That lets your customer know
you've heard them.

Rule 164

If you're not funny, don't try to be.

We all have strengths. If comedy is not yours, don't force it.

Rule 165

interrupt

If you ask a question, let the person finish their answer.

Otherwise why did you ask?

Rule 166

Don't give me a guided tour of your house like it's a museum.

Only if the guests ask for a tour.

Rule 167

**If someone stops you on the street
and recognizes you, always say
thank you for saying hello.**

Former President George H.W. Bush
was known for this.

Rule 168

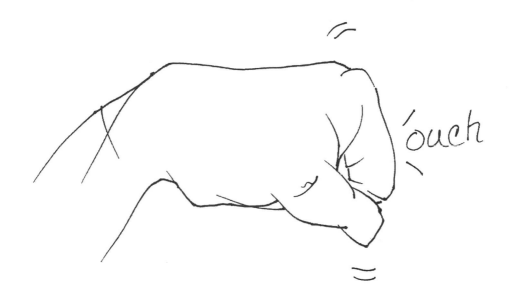

Don't grab me from behind or slap me on the back, and don't punch me in the arm.

Playing this physical game
is for third graders.

Rule 169

Parking rules apply to you, big shot.

Handicap spots, double parking laws, and
fire zones exist for a reason.

Rule 170

There are three areas where you will not change someone's mind:

Politics, favorite baseball team, and sex.

Rule 171

If you have to look at your phone, apologize before you do it.

Don't stare at it and nod distractedly while I continue to talk.

Rule 172

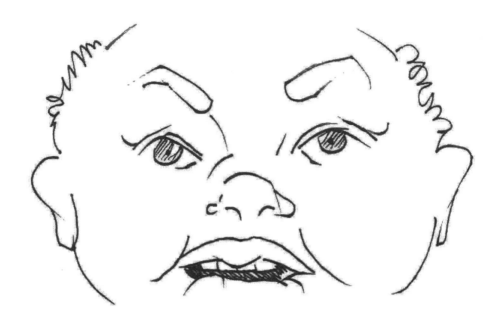

**Be careful of your facial expressions
when people are speaking to you.**

If you're bored or annoyed when talking to
someone, try the poker face.

Rule 173

Don't play with your fork while someone is talking to you at dinner.

Nothing says "I'm bored" like fidgeting with your flatware.

Rule 174

Don't rush into elevators.

Someone could be coming out.
This is "breaking news"—Sometimes
people are in the elevator about to exit.

Rule 175

**Call your clients on the weekends
for no reason.**

It shows you're thinking about them,
even when you don't have to be.

Rule 176

Acknowledge a text or email.

A simple "got it" or "received" will do.

Rule 177

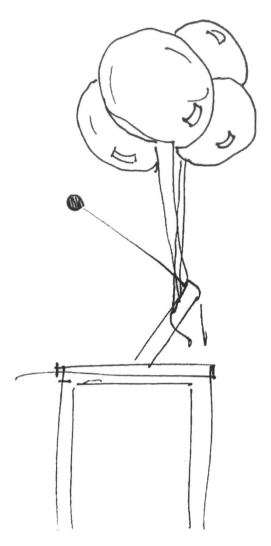

**If you're not the keynote speaker,
don't act like it.**

If you are the warm-up act,
don't overplay your role.

Rule 178

If you ask me to speak, don't introduce me by saying "Jon Bramnick wants to say a few words."

You invited me, not the other way around.

Rule 179

In social sports like golf, don't be the "rules judge."

Don't call people out on little-known rules. You'll quickly find yourself playing alone.

Rule 180

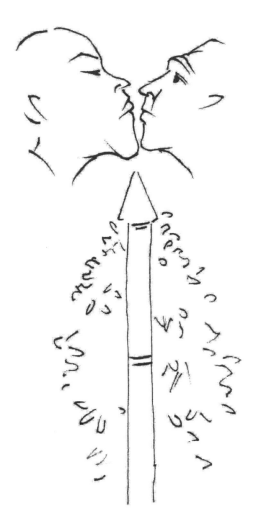

Fights with your neighbors
are always bad.

You have to live in the same neighborhood.
You don't need the headache. This creates
incredible stress every single day.

Rule 181

If anyone asks you to help their children, ALWAYS say yes.

You can't go wrong helping someone's child. Not only do you earn goodwill from the parents, but parents will never forget it.

Rule 182

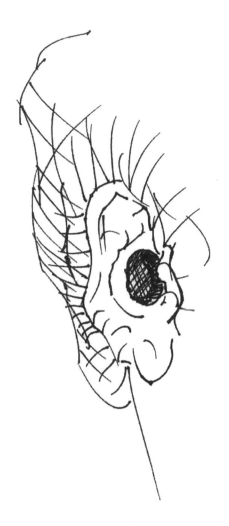

Take the Bluetooth out of your ear when you are talking to me.

Very annoying that you may be listening to someone else. It also looks stupid.

Rule 183

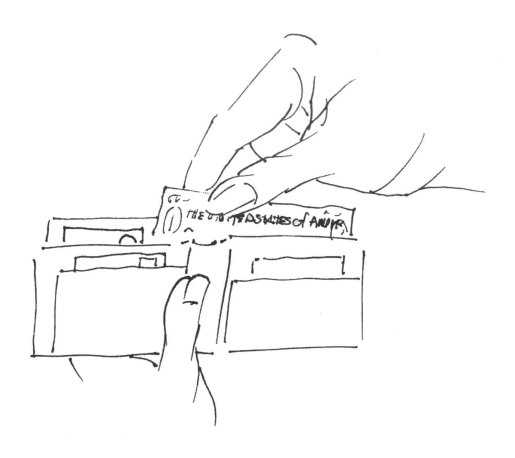

**Don't repack your purse or wallet
while I'm standing behind you in line.**

While you replace 900 items into your
wallet, my ice cream is melting and my
milk is getting warm.

Rule 184

Take your wallet out and be ready to pay before the clerk finishes ringing you up.

You know you're going to be asked for money; get your wallet out ahead of time and save the people behind you a few seconds.

Rule 185

**Don't send your annual letter
bragging about your family.**

Rule 186

Saying anything negative to another person, even in jest, doesn't play well.

You are insulting the person,
and it ain't funny.

Rule 187

The relationship is always more important than winning the argument.

Great. You were right. But now your friend won't talk to you.

Rule 188

Ask people for their advice.

It shows them you respect their opinion.

Rule 189

Congratulate people who have received an honor by sending a note or text.

A simple acknowledgment of someone's success goes a long way.

Rule 190

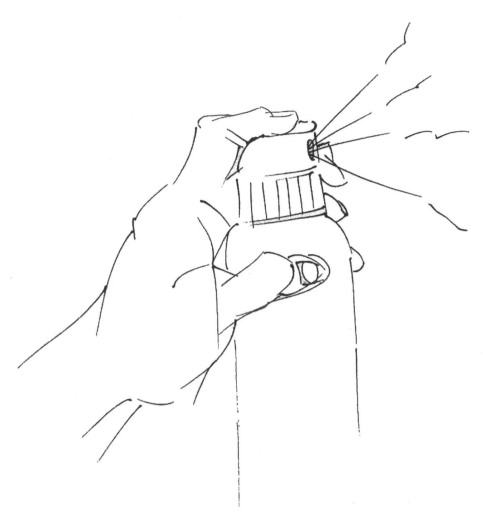

Don't spray your suntan lotion on while you're standing next to me.

That stuff is poison. If you want to breathe it, go for it, just don't force me to breathe it too.

Rule 191

Don't fight with your spouse in public.

Your friends don't want to have to judge
who is right and who is wrong.

Rule 192

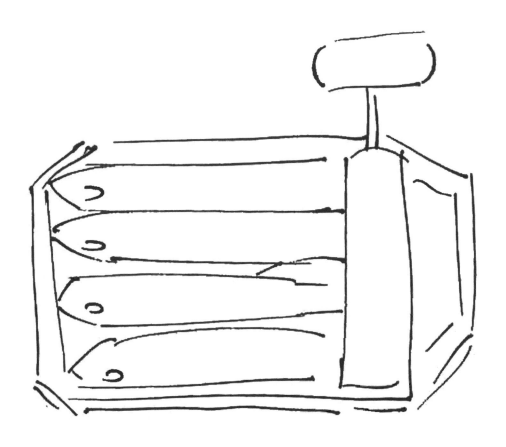

Don't eat pungent food when you're sitting near someone.

Eat your sardines in a private room, or better yet, leave them at home.

Rule 193

Do not eat while you are talking on the phone. The crunching of food is disrespectful to the other party.

Swallow your food before dialing.

Rule 194

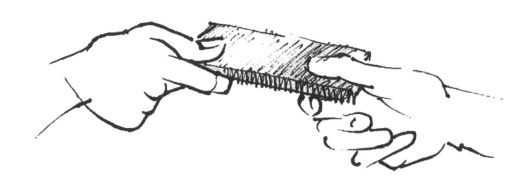

When offering to pick up the tab, do not say "Let me buy." That is weak.

Instead say "I will pay for this."

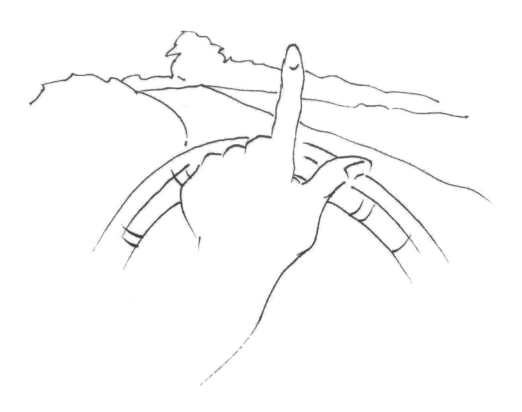

**When you are driving and you have
passengers, look at the road during
a conversation. I hear you.
Also don't drive with only
one finger on the steering wheel,
and DON'T TAILGATE.**

You can do all of the above
when I am not in your car.

Rule 196

Don't complain about high-class problems.

"I hate the place because they do not have old French wines." "The first class on United Airlines does not give you the warm hand towels."

Rule 197

Call people for no reason; checking in.

Don't always call with an "ask."

Rule 198

Don't slurp your coffee.

Disgusting.

Rule 199

**Don't let your 7-year-old child
call me by my first name
unless I authorize it.**

Rule 200

Don't leave your car running
while you run into the coffee shop.

Rule 201

Don't save seats at the pool, asshole.

Rule 202

When on a plane don't put your seat all the way back.

I understand that the seat goes all the way back, but it is not mandatory to place the back of your seat in my face.

Rule 203

Don't write books that criticize everyone's behavior.

Rule 204

Don't take books like this too seriously.

I have violated every rule in this book and continue to violate them, although I try not to.

Rule 205